the captain asks for
a show of hands

books by nick flynn

Some Ether

A Note Slipped under the Door (coauthored with Shirley McPhillips)

Blind Huber

Another Bullshit Night in Suck City

Alice Invents a Little Game and Alice Always Wins

The Ticking Is the Bomb

The Captain Asks for a Show of Hands

The Reenactments

the captain asks for
a show of hands

poems

nick flynn

graywolf press

This publication is made possible, in part, by the voters of Minnesota through a Minnesota State Arts Board Operating Support grant, thanks to a legislative appropriation from the arts and cultural heritage fund, and through a grant from the National Endowment for the Arts. Significant support has also been provided by Target, the McKnight Foundation, Amazon.com, and other generous contributions from foundations, corporations, and individuals. To these organizations and individuals we offer our heartfelt thanks.

Published by Graywolf Press
250 Third Avenue North, Suite 600
Minneapolis, Minnesota 55401

www.graywolfpress.org

Published in the United States of America

ISBN 978-1-55597-574-6 (cloth)
ISBN 978-1-55597-633-0 (paper)

2 4 6 8 9 7 5 3 1

Library of Congress Control Number: 2012949112

Cover design: Scott Sorenson

Cover photo: Kahn & Selesnick, *King of Birds*

manifest

one

two

three

the captain asks for

        a show of hands

. . . a spokesman can only / state his surprise
that it doesn't happen more often . . .

one

haiku (failed)

The thin thread that holds us here, tethered / or maybe tied, together, what / do you call it—*telephone? horizon? song?* Listen / to yourself sing, *We are all god's children* / we are all gods, we walk the earth / sometimes, two sails inside us sometimes / beating, our bodies the bottle, a ship inside each / until one day, for no reason, it sails— *hello?* / damn phone—until one day it sails / out of sight, until one day it cuts out of / earshot, bye-bye muttered into your cupped palm, *bye-bye* / *boat, bye-bye rain*—Look / maybe this is the place we've been / waiting for, maybe this place / is the day, inside us, inside each / corpuscle, the day, that day, everyday is / inside, my body, your body, everyday is / this thread, everyday you said, *come* / *get me,* everyday you said, *it's been way too long* / you said, *bye-bye,* bye-bye, not a day / went by, the thin, the thread, so thin, this thread, are you still / here, is it still, your heart, is it well, well, welling?

fire

more the idea of the flame than the flame
as in: the flame

of the rose petal, the flame of the thorn
the sun is a flame, the dog's teeth

flames

to be clear: with the body,

capt'n, we can do as we wish, we can do
as we wish with the body

but we cannot leave marks—capt'n I'm
trying to get this right

the world's so small, the sky so high
we pray for rain it rains, we pray for sun it suns

we pray on our knees, we move our lips
we pray in our minds, we clasp our hands

our hands look tied before us

I remember, capt'n, something, it
didn't happen, not

to me—this guy, I knew him by
face, I don't remember his

name, one night
walking home from a party, a car it

clipped him, for hours he
wandered, dazed, his family, his

neighbors, with flashlights they
searched, all night, the woods

calling out

here's the part, capt'n, where I tell a story
as if it were a confession: I was hiding out on

damon rock, lighting
matches & letting them drop to the leaves

below—little flare-

ups, flash fires—a girl wandered
down the path, she just

stood there, watching the matches
fall from my hand—

capt'n, I'm trying to be precise: hot

day, a cage in the sun, a room without
air, the mind-bending heat, the music

a flame—*hey*
metallica hey britney hey airless hey fuse, I

don't know how it happened, perched far
above, I offered her a match

to pull down her pants, one
match, her hairless

body, hey

little girl, I dropped it unlit—
I didn't know what it was I was looking at

hey capt'n I don't know if I'm allowed
hey capt'n years ago I'm walking

one drunk night, even now I
wonder—sometimes still I

imagine—was I hit am I
dazed, this

dream this confession, hey
little girl is your daddy home, hey capt'n hey

sir am I making any sense?

the boy stood on the burning deck, stammering
elocution, wait—
the boy stood in the burning cage, stammering
electrocution, no—the boy stood in the hot-hot room
stammering I did stammering I did stammering I
did stammering I did stammering everything you say I did
I did

hey metallica hey britney hey airless hey fuse
hey phonograph hey hades hey thoughtless hey

capt'n this room is on fire

capt'n this body will not stop burning

capt'n oh my captain this burning has become a body

capt'n oh my captain this child is ash

capt'n oh my captain my hands pass right through her

capt'n oh my captain I don't know what it is I'm looking at

it's important to be precise, to say what
I know—

the sun is fire, the center of the earth
is fire, yr mother's cunt is

fire, an airless flame, still, still, I don't know why
she pushed me out, this cold cold furnace, we all

were pushed, a rim of light around our heads, she
gave a kick, sent us crawling

out, toward the flame, toward the pit, the flaming
pit, yr lover's tongue, the flame

a thorn

everyday, capt'n, sir, captain, I was
left, a child, after school, alone, I found

a match, under the sink I found a can, a spray
can, *ly-sol dis-infectant*, it made a

torch, I was careful the flame didn't
enter the can, I knew it

would explode, somehow I knew, I'm
trying to be clear, sir—the flame

shot across the room, then it was gone

false prophet

The book tells us to cling (cling?) / to the thought that, in god's /
hands, our dark past is our greatest / possession (*You've ruined it,* the
woman with / the riding crop says to the man on all / fours, naked
but for his mask—*pigs don't talk*). Cling— / maybe inside this word
are more words, maybe / inside darkness is simply more darkness.
God's / hands? Here's a riddle—a cosmonaut / holds hands with an
astronaut, both un- / tethered. Which one is confusing a pinpoint of
light / with an unreachable planet?

jesus knew

unlike you & I   jesus knew he'd die

some days a headache woke him   it

lingered   nothing terrible   but the word

hung around his temples like this

soul everyone wants but can't find   jesus

knew he'd die   he just didn't know how

& that bothered him sometimes   & then

he'd do one of his little   tricks

what the hell   didn't hurt anyone

didn't make anyone disappear for-

ever but the tricks   stopped working he forgot

why he did them & what for he confused

a story about a guy named jesus

with a story about a father he never knew

& it all began to hang like a moth-eaten coat

pulled out of a trunk on a shaky day hey   let's

return to the scene of the fucken tragedy   at least

we all know how it turns out   instead of this endless

uncertainty   hey

let's sell our souls a few more

times   no one's really counting   (those

little papers you trade for your sins   what

do you call them?   *anyone?*

no?)   —anyway—jesus

this   jesus that   god of nickel

god of dime   right

the real jesus he was   lost he   walked in-
to the desert   not far really   his friends his
disciples   he told them he'd come back
like us he said this every time he left but jesus
never said wait never pointed to the sky
never claimed he'd rise again never asked us to eat
his flesh jesus   never asked for anything   as far
as I can tell   he got tired everyday & then slept
sometimes okay   sometimes un-
bearable   the dreams   the father
pointing a finger at everyone   a finger we can't
even look at

air

we put them in cages they don't like the cages
we put them in cells they pray

I swim in the palace it rains from the sky
the pool between palm tree & wall

the air in the cells is poison they claim
the air in the cages is dust

I sink to the bottom to see what it's like
a grave in the air where you won't lie too cramped

space monkey, suffocation
roulette—*super-*

cali-fragilistic-hyperventilation,
super-cali-fragilistic-cali-

fornication—squat
down breathe in breathe out thirty

times fast like this (*breathe*) your
buddy behind you stand his arms

lift your feet from the floor his arms
squeeze all the air out—black-

out fallout all out over &
out—then nirvana then nothing then

capt'n I'd lay at his feet I'd have myself
finally I'd have myself my little

dream my little *shine on you crazy*
diamond dog day afternoon delight

the palace on fire it clouds up the sky
I hate the sound of their prayers

I swim underwater I empty my lungs
if you think about breathing you can't

the palace still burning a cloud in the air
their mats in a row the mark on their heads

a grave in the air where you won't lie too cramped
they don't have wings so we lift them

before modest mouse capt'n what
was the world, what was the world

before pavement?

before I was nothing I was silence before
before I was here I was no one

the radio one day it made me of air
a soundtrack to walk down these halls

we'll all float on okay okay
we'll all float on okay

they scream my lieutenant he calls it a song
I want them to sing he says louder

I wish you could hear the soundtrack we play
for hours & naked they dance

I take out my camera I capture the sound
at first it was weird then it wasn't

before there's a song there's a day it just isn't
before there's a photo it's dark

& we'll all float on okay okay
& we'll all float on okay

something is wrong with the air in the cells
capt'n something is wrong with the air

the prisoner capt'n his lips gone all blue
capt'n something is wrong with the air

maybe our bodies are no more than jars
meant to hold what we name *everything*

airplane photograph leash glove & song
it all pours in with each breath

often I am permitted to return to a desert
often I am permitted to bleed

then someone hands me their darkness in rags
then someone sits on my chest

oblivion nothing emptiness night
it helps to think it's a game

play let-your-mind-wander, play stoned-porno-drift

play pop-pop-pop-popping, play oh-what-is-this
play look-down-touch-your-chest, play hole-in-your-vest

play air-puffing-out, play fall-to-your-knees
pretend to fall to your knees

capt'n this morning six were found hanging
in a room made completely of air

they knotted their blankets their blankets dissolved
& their necks stretched to the floor

& yesterday capt'n thirty stopped eating
I forget the words to this song

we feed them with tubes their vitals are good
it helps to think it's a game

& we'll all float on okay okay
& we'll all float on okay

here is your bowl of steam capt'n
here's your syringe of sky

here is the why & the pop pop pop pop
of the gun you will never see

if you focus on breathing the world will spin right
the mouthful you lose trying to save

& here is the doer & here's the done-to
& the jar that will send us all home

imagination

The ground's not a bad place
to live for a while, a few

years, not face-
down, exactly, not

faceup either—hovering, say,
over the dirt, the earth

is dirt, our bodies dirt & you
floating there, a hand's-

width above me, just until
things blow over, that

war, say, *jesus,*
did we really just make it all up?

two

greetings, friend (minotaur)

O heart weighed down by so many wings / isn't it time to admit / we are more machinery than gods / that our house is more maze than temple, that contrary / to popular mechanics we cannot, anytime / simply change the channel. Bashō / year after year, saw on the monkey's face / a monkey face. Here we are, friend, year out / year in, in our bodies, inside them, seemingly, everything / as promised, ten percent off. You say / *the family car was always warming up.* You say / *wasn't there a tv show about a minotaur?* You say / *O heart weighed down by so many wings, where / is my monkey mask now?*

kedge

ceaselessly, I said, let's hold each other / ceaselessly
your bed a box cut out of the sky

what I meant was *inescapably* / the sky about to collapse
upon us. I can't feel my body, I said

I meant, with you I can't feel my body *ending*
your bed's not empty / will never be, not ever

this wall's not a floor / the tub's not a bomb
the window's not a river of light to wade / please

can we start again—say

sorry dear ocean dear desperate dear boat
sorry dear shoulder dear caveman

please hand me a match / please speak of the flame
please speak as it moves down its body

please name where to touch / please say the word *ear*
say *stone* say *under my tongue*

the sun it feels good as it shadows your face
my neck still cold where you kiss it

the bowl never empties / never darkens or fills / your body
fits into each breath

the ocean inside you / our palms never touch
the boat of a name we call lost

say *not* become holy / say *won't* then keep turning
say empty your pockets upon me

unable inside you / your lips seal the hull
unable inside before sleep

past mudflats paced-out / past islands unmapped
past mirrors that go on without us

each shorelight a window / each window a mouth
the harbor a throat without reason

make up a reason as yet understood
all night to kedge my ass homeward

the baffled king composing hallelujah

Jubilee, our war's almost over (again), we ship out / tomorrow (again) / back to wherever it was / we began (again)—photographs stuck to the fridge, a red plastic / donut underfoot, a bathtub filling (amen). Close your eyes—where are you / right now, what city—no? / Nothing? Krishna, trying / to convince Arjuna of the righteousness of / battle, boiled it down to eleven words /—*We'll never untangle the circumstances that brought us / to this moment.* Still nowhere? Here's another hint—my hands are not / inside you, your hands are not / inside me, & one of us has forgotten / how to breathe. We created a wasteland (*bye-bye*) / & called it peace.

earth

last night I wandered, capt'n, the earth
bright & poison, I

staggered, a forced march, yes, then
digging, a grave, made to dig my own

grave, someone muttered *kiss
my ass*, a body walked into the

earth, I saw my own body, covering itself
with earth, my body becoming

earth

if I understand the memo right, capt'n, we can use

water, but we cannot use earth—that is,

we can simulate drowning, but not

burial—is that right, sir,

capt'n? I've read

the memos & I want to do

what's right

muhammed, ahmed, achmed, whatever
here we are—me & you & these

walls again, fifteen feet thick—packed earth

baked earth scorched earth & out-
side these walls the sand, on

fire, yes, still, & oh
yes, my question, my one simple

question—look at me,
do you think I want to be here any more than you?

capt'n: the memo says we cannot bury

the prisoner, but does that mean we can bury his

son? I mean, does it say we can *pretend* to bury his son?

capt'n, does the memo say we cannot pretend to bury

the prisoner's son, does it say we cannot make the prisoner

dig his son's grave, does it say we cannot make the prisoner

place his son in the hole? I'm trying, capt'n,

& he has still not answered my question

a spigot, a hose, a floor-drain
dead center—it drains into

the earth, the sand, somewhere out there, out-
side these walls—you can smell it, your

face pressed to the tile, it tastes like
tile you think it tastes like your village you

think all tile you think all tile you

think all tile you think baked
earth scorched earth hospital

yellow yolk yellow dead yellow
sulphur yellow

that dream again, capt'n, as soon as my eyes
shut—the one where the car goes into a skid

& I can't pull out, the one where I wipe my ass
but the paper never comes clean

hello, birdy

paint a hungry bird / paint its cage black
paint a tunnel scraped out with a spoon

paint a sign in a window / *free bird with each cage*
black letters burnt through a white board

paint the bird as she sings / paint each bar in her cage
worthless the song that she sings

her feathers are black / her blood it is black
black beak black cage black song

hello birdy / hello black wings
black eye pressed to the bars

well well welling / peckity peckity peck
the dirt carried out in your beak

forgetting something

Try this—close / your eyes. No, wait, when—if—we see each other /
again, the first thing we should do is close our eyes—no, / first we
should tie our hands to something / solid—bedpost, doorknob—
otherwise they (wild birds) / might startle us / awake. Are we forget-
ting something? What about that / warehouse, the one beside the
airport, that room / of black boxes, a man in each box? If you / bring
this one into the light he will not stop / crying, if you show this one
a photo of his son / his eyes go dead. Turn up / the heat, turn up the
song. First thing we should do / if we see each other again is to make /
a cage of our bodies—inside we can place / whatever still shines.

almost song

Still the voice starts when I open

my mouth, first it's breath
then air then sky

If the wind shakes the tree then cut the tree down
If the cow moves then shoot her

I open to speak, the sky

tumbles out, this thirty-year
song, this cloud for a head, assume it

comes out of my mouth. One mucky

boot, what to make of a mouth
when each day rebuilds

the shape of a ditch, the body
gone missing below

A body no more, a dog on the block
maybe eaten or not, with only one sun

with each morning worse (your
giddy-up hearse)

the road blown to shit, not quicklime

not thatch
worse to open to say, to lower the sky

a dog on the block, eaten or not
its paws for sale knotted with twine.

Bleeding out into sleep, this song
that prays night, I pretend I've been

hit, it comes from my mouth

the sky or the air, not blue anymore
& riverstones rising like helmets

self-exam (my body is a cage)

Do this: take two fingers, push them into
the spot behind your ear, the spot

your skull drops off

into that valley of muscle
& nerve—this is the muscle that holds up

the skull, that nods the dumb bone
this way & that

when you think you under-
stand, when you think you get it—press deeper

into the gristle, find that little bundle of
nerves—the nerves

that make you blink at day-

light, that make your tongue slide in &
out when you think you're in

love, when you think you need a drink, touch
that spot as if you had an itch
as if it were a button, as if you were

an elevator, close your eyes &

listen, please, close
your eyes—can you hear it? We think our souls live

in boxes, we think someone sits behind our eyes,
lording from his little throne, steering the fork to

the mouth, the mouth to the tit, we think hungry
children live in our bellies, clutching their empty

bowls as the food rains
down, we sometimes think we are those

hungry children, we think
we can think anything & it won't

matter, we think we can think *cut out her tongue,*
then ask her to sing

water

night & prison & desert & darkness
a pipe, a sewer, a river

after the thorn the prisoner broke
no—after the storm the survivor spoke

I didn't know what the water wanted

$30K, base pay, just for
signing, but it's easy to

bump it up—carry a gun,
boom, hazard

pay—carry a gun outside the green
zone, *boom*—work the prison night

shift, *boom*—
boom, boom, boom

back home, capt'n, I was always on
lookout, any

bridge, any ledge I could

dive from, the highest point
to throw my body off

of—bridge, quarry, waterfall

nothing to flood, drymouth to
drowning, everyone's here for a purpose

my girl, capt'n, four fingers in her
mouth, she'd lick them, drop

by drop by drop by drop, until her hand
glistened, she'd cup it down

anywhere, the water whispers, everything
wet, an oasis in the near dark

here comes the tub, here comes the board
here comes the cloth, here comes the bucket

on an empty road, capt'n, I found a bridge
the river pure & black below

step out of your body step off into

nothing—capt'n,
I knew I'd be here by christmas

press an ear to the wall—water inside the wall
water is the empty tub, water is

a licked tile, a grain of sand
one drop hangs on the prisoner's tongue—capt'n,

are we allowed to force him to swallow?

a car, a tree stump, the wall of a ruined
house—stories, capt'n, sub-

merged in the rain-filled
quarries, gone

for years

sometimes, some-
how, break free, rise up

something, capt'n, is
wrong, this one stopped

breathing—they said he wouldn't
drown

then he drowned

water asks a question, water holds on
while it asks a question, it's hard

to understand water's question

come with me, water says, the city
burning outside your walls

invasion of the body snatchers

A child (somewhere) squats, scratches / the dirt with a twig, muttering *broken broken / broken* muttering *an excellent place to hide* / an excellent hole, a hidey-hole, a spider hole, the hole she / will crawl into or through one day, not / today, thank god, not yet, she can't know yet / each hole is a word, each word / a thread. Let's try this again, without / the child this time—*broken broken broken* / no sun today, no shadow. Tiring / isn't it, this kneeling, lips pressed to / the sidewalk, whispering into a crack. *Yesterday / it all seemed normal,* Brooke Adams says / to Donald Sutherland, as he drives her to / the psychiatrist—*today everything seemed the same / but it wasn't.* Brooke didn't know, couldn't / know, not then, that Donald was gone / already gone.

oh here

are his teeth, now
lodged in my head, oh here

is his scrawl, coming out of
my hand

& here is a thought
that passed through his

mind, when I open

my mouth he never
shuts up. Once was

a spider, exploded

inside him, once was a hole
no shovel to fill. Oh here

is the jacket that held him
together, & here are

his breasts, sagging off of
my chest. The jacket he

wore, attempting

to nurse me, the bruise of
his nipple, un-

buttoned his heart. Oh
here is his box, but he's only

sleeping, I'll take you
some night, I'll show you

his spots, I'll buy you
a token, we'll ride under-

ground, I'll show you a tooth
the last I could find, I'll

show you a stain, it proves
        he was here

three

seven testimonies (redacted)

I woke up, I asked why—
my children, my

wife, my leg. Outside
my head—cold, rainy,

a tent—there were others
I heard,

my brother, a pipe, cold
water at night. They let me

go once, my hands always
laughing

broomstick was I was
you are we want—

one better one blanket
for under & one

& fifteen days of food. One man had
a heart, a pill under

his tongue—a pill, a dog,

a broomstick. They knew I
was someone

& my house was on
luck—they gave me

summer, we threw stones
& peed

That night in that tent, one
on each side,

the photographer

lifted the ground. The next day
to Garso, a cold tank of

water (sometimes

with ice), they were going
& coming

& then they went
back—I tried to find myself

all night

A dark room, a beard
men with

beards, who looked
like I remember. I

remember
waking up, somewhere

a dog, I remember
those days, two others

were there, I remember
two days

laughing

One night I
woke up, started

giving, started
getting, after one

three more. Forty

days later & he was the one—
he left me

part of the gate

a farmer I was, twenty-two
on the ground—hands

feet back fists & blood.
Nine days I was

I walked naked in front

the door closed to breathe
the door opened a crack

the third day would want
the third day she want

my hand stretched to kiss
electric until

I could see my arm &
was still

My eyesight is years
I see up yes did this

Yes you this I saw
A sister you see

In the showers you this
In this with yes I

Was naked you this
Yes to me & wanted

dear lady of perpetual something

Just now I thought something about
the body

about your body, how it goes on

& on, unspooling. Dear Something
Dear Nothing, if

(one day) I write about painting myself
into a corner—*I have lived so much*

with you not being here—I might
find myself, in fact, painted into

a corner

Behind my eyes a lake of fire
Behind your head a birdless sky

Here is the wine, here are the christened
Illinoise snowfall, wires that glisten

My blindfold? My curtain? My darkness? Your wings?
The song in my head is *Burn Down the Mission.*

Dear Lady of Something Dear Lady
of Nothing

look up—that airplane, my body in-
side it, your Nashville

below—a thousand gems, a thousand
bodies, each

gilded with spit. Dear Lady

Dear Sailor, is that your body, lying in that
field, moaning softly

the field constructed entirely of
words? Look up, wave

your broken fingers, take off your boots
—lucky you, held at last

Once upon a time, when you were being born
the doctor stuck her fingers

up your mother's ass—*here box*

here open here door—to guide your head
through. . . . By the way,

the light beside the bed, imagine it
dimmed by a blue

scarf, imagine the field
bathed in sunlight, imagine shadows

underfoot

e. corpse

Red red flash, red red dress, red the chimera's,

the camaro's, red crash. If I cut out a card-
board mother, if I cut out a cardboard gun

cardboard cunt & cardboard pill
& a childproof ocean of spit

a cardboard boat & its cardboard fire–looky
look: this little piggy ate

roast beef, this little piggy ate
none (that can't be

right). Thursday's child is
bound to crash, Friday's child is ashes

ash. . . . Once

(yesterday?) I swung
a dishtowel in my daughter's path—what does

the bullfighter say? *En garde? Toro*
toro toro? I wanted her to see, no—I wanted her

to be, to become

a bull. Instead, she opened the bathroom door
with a tiny elephant. O holy Chinese city of tiny

elephants—I'll take you one

day, I swear, before all the planes fall from
the sky. O

look—the sun again, everywhere, at

once. O my monkey of the fading dark, arms
upraised—a word,

not yet a word, climbing out of your little cage.

pulse (hidden bird)

Imagine a glass of water, a drop of blood / suspended, dead / center—
one drop, watch it / dissolve. I can't tell the difference, not today,
not / really, between this & / your body, faceup, in a pond, say, eyes
closed, each pulsing / leaf. What else / are we here for, why are we
this / & not nothing, you know, the big questions—& / what about
our dead, what do we do / with them, we have to turn them in-/
to something, right? Mine / never came back, mine keep coming /
back, please, I beg you, open / your eyes, please, open your mouth,
or let me / open it, please, there's something I need / to taste. It's so
simple—lurking inside us is / a child, a real child, running with
both / hands in the air, as if escaping a prison, laughing / now, the
wall far behind her

saudade

this boat, this broken boat—*beam, stem, keel,*
oar—this beach littered with broken

boats—broken beam

broken stem broken keel broken oar
this head littered with broken eyes this mouth

littered with broken teeth
rot stench mold stench tooth stench

gone. I
pass a woman on the street, we slept together

once, a night too stormy to row
back out—

the tower towers above us

now, we can see it
from wherever, it gives the impression

we will never get lost

between outside & inside
here (salt on

the deck, sand on your neck)—

between inside & outside here
there never was

much difference. Some mornings
the fog, a red plastic

bucket, only that telephone pole
to pull us along. Mollie's house-

boat broke loose last night, bumped
the shore (mine

needs paint). The tide
will be a foot lower tomorrow, a foot

lower the day after that &
so on until the new

moon, when it will all tilt, spill, pour, flood (*flood
tide*) back. We cannot

not think of it. Say this:

always, in each lit room, say I'd see them,
nights I didn't

(couldn't) make it to shore

Oysters.

A pool table in the basement—whatever
drops overboard, whatever you

bury, whatever is

abandoned, rises up, washes
up, will all, eventually, be

salvage. Ashore, glance up
to the tops of the trees—see how their leaves

move. I'd meant to put her back in the next spring,
but something

happened. Gulls sometimes (sometimes
just a drawing of a gull),

the sky still blue, cover
the high school field, thousands of

them—all of them, seemingly—

there is a boat which is no more
a boat, beside a house

which is no more a house, in a town which is no
more a town—we no longer

say hello, no longer seem to even see
each other. I wonder now

whether we'd ever been together
at all

The leaf dropped from the branch

The seed rolled onto the deck
The seedling pushed into the caulking

The sapling split the plank
The tree lifts her into the fog—*beam, stem, keel, oar*—

this boat, this broken boat, this beach
littered with broken boats—*We have come back*

from Jerusalem where we found
not what we sought

[some notes]

haiku (failed)
The poem contains a line from the Kinks song "God's Children."

fire
The poem contains lines pulled or twisted from the following sources: Elizabeth Bishop ("Casabianca"); Galway Kinnell (*The Book of Nightmares*); Hart Crane (*The Bridge*); Walt Whitman ("O Captain! My Captain!"); and Bruce Springsteen ("I'm on Fire"). The "Britney" is Ms. Spears, one of the artists (along with Metallica, and dozens more) whose music was used, without permission, to torture prisoners in Abu Ghraib and elsewhere—ASCAP is pressing the US military for royalty payments.

false prophet
The line in parentheses is from Roman Polanski's *Bitter Moon*.

jesus knew
The poem borrows a gesture from the Will Eno play *Thom Paine (About Nothing)*.

air
The poem contains lines pulled or twisted from the following sources: Paul Celan ("Deathfugue"); Modest Mouse ("Float On"); Robert Duncan ("Often I Am Permitted to Return to a Meadow").

greetings, friend (minotaur)
O heart weighed down by so many wings is the one-line poem "Artichoke," in its entirety, by Joseph Hutchinson.

the baffled king composing hallelujah
The title is from the Leonard Cohen song "Hallelujah," and the poem also contains lines from Tacitus and the Bhagavad Gita.

almost song
The poem was written after a trip to Vietnam with my stepfather, John Mattson, in 1999, where we worked on the documentary film

Breathe In, Breathe Out, directed by Beth B., which is about American veterans of the Vietnam War and their children. The lines in italics are from another documentary film of the Vietnam War, the name of which is lost to me now.

self-exam (my body is a cage)
"My Body Is A Cage" is an Arcade Fire song.

water
i. The line "I didn't know what the water wanted" is lifted from Claudia Rankine's poem "Backed Up in the Soul (collected from CNN)." It was spoken by a survivor of Hurricane Katrina, immediately after the storm.
ii. Phillipe Sands, in *The Torture Team*, documents a CIA spook's response to a soldier's question about the proper method to waterboard someone—*If he dies, you're doing it wrong.*

seven testimonies (redacted)
The poems in this series are redacted versions of the testimonies of seven Abu Ghraib detainees, as transcribed by the artist Daniel Heyman, in Amman and in Istanbul, from 2006–2008. I was present for those testimonies gathered in 2007, in Istanbul. The testimonies, as transcribed by Heyman, are as follows:

1

It was three a.m. and I woke up with a soldier at the door to my bedroom. I asked why he was here and he hit my head. I heard soldiers hitting my children, my family. Even they beat up my wife, and broke my son's leg. He was eleven. I was taken outside, and a hood was put on my head, and tied my hands. I heard my family screaming. What happened next? They took me to a cage. It was cold, rainy. It was in a tent, and there were other detainees in cages. I was dragged. I heard my brother speaking. Why are we here? I was in the cage seven days. They hit me with a pipe through the top of the cage. They threw cold water on us at night, and poked me with a skewer. They let me go to the bathroom once in seven days. My hands were always cuffed. They were laughing.

2

The broomstick was metal. I was hit in the face, back, legs at Abu Ghraib. They said, We know that you are innocent, but we want to scare the Iraqi people. At camp one, Abu Ghraib, conditions were better. We had one blanket for under me, and one to cover myself. During the fifteen days of Falujah Battle, they cut our food to held a ration every two days. One man from Dialah Province had a heart condition. One night he asked the guards for a pill to put under his tongue. They did not give him a pill and he died that night. They took his body away. They released a dog on me. It bit my pants. Then the interpreter hit me for ten minutes with a stick, a broomstick. He said you Iraqis do not deserve life, Muslims do not deserve life. They said they knew I was innocent but they needed someone from the area, and my house was on the main street. Bad luck. To get to Tarik, they woke me at three a.m.. It was January and they gave me summer clothes. We were made to crouch in the truck. They threw stones at us and peed on us. We were all hooded. The trip lasted from four a.m. until six p.m.

3

Then I went to Abu Ghraib for twenty-two days. There is one other thing that happened at Garso but I cannot talk about it. I did not have a beard. I even enjoy drinking. I am not a religious man. That night in that tent they put bombs between my legs, and rifles around me. Two. One on each side, and then the photographers took pictures. The bomb was real. Then they started asking me questions. They put a rope around my right wrist and tied the rope around a pipe and lifted me off the ground by this arm for three hours. I still have problems lifting my arm. The next day they took me to Garso. There they put me in a hole with water. Next they took my clothing. They would take us at four in the morning and put us in a cold tank of water, sometimes with ice. They were hitting us and beating us going and coming, and then they went back to their cells in cold wet clothes. I tried to find some way to kill myself. This was for all six nights.

4

They took me to a dark room. I had a beard. They said they were after men with beards, who looked like Bin Laden. I remember two days later waking up somewhere else with a dog barking at me. I don't remember those days. Two other detainees were also there. They said they were raped. I don't remember those two days. The soldiers were laughing in a sarcastic way and said that they had raped me.

5

On the way to the toilet they would beat me. Then they would count to five and I would have to pee in those five seconds. No one told me why I was arrested. One night I woke up and a soldier was urinating on us. The guards would molest a young prisoner, touching his penis, taking him to the toilet. At Abu Ghraib they chose five of us and they started giving us injections. I had five injections. I started to forget after getting the shots. After one year. Before leaving they gave me three more shots. Forty days later. They told me they were vaccines. I feel my head is heavy. We refused to take these vaccinations, we tried to resist. They took me to the interrogation at Abu Ghraib in a Humvee, and they took my hood off. They asked me questions and took me away. They kicked me and insulted me on the way back. The second interrogation was more violent. The translator was a big Egyptian. He was a mean person. He was tall and he was the one who beat me. He smashed my face to the wall. The next interrogation was more difficult. They hit me and kicked me on the way. This was the guards. They left me alone for one hour, and then the interrogation. At Abu Ghraib the camp was bombed. We took the body parts of the dead prisoners to the front gates of the camp.

6

I am a farmer. I was twenty-two at the time of the arrest. In the interrogation I was forced on the ground. My hands tied to my feet behind my back. The interpreter hit me with his fists and kick me with his army boots. I vomited blood. For nine days I was not allowed to leave the cell and use the bathroom.

Then I was sent to Abu Ghraib in a hood. They told me to undress. I removed all but my underwear. I was taken to the showers and forced to take off my under wear. The hood was put back on and I was walked to a cell naked, in front of others with a hood. With the cell door closed it was hard to breathe. One meter by four meters, and I had no food for three days. The door was opened a crack once an hour. Another detainee said that the third day a female soldier would want to have sex with me. The third day, a male and female soldier came and he said she want (sic) to have sex with me. I refused, Islam does not allow this. Then they tied my hand outstretched, and the female soldier started to kiss me and tried to have sex with me, touched me where she should not—I spat at her. They left and other soldiers came in, beat me with sticks, and then put an electric shock until I could not see and passed out. They broke my left arm and my right leg. I was still tied up and naked.

7

My eyesight is fading. In a few years I will be blind. Did you ever see prisoners piled up like this? Yes. Did this happen to you? Yes. Do you recognize this woman? Yes, I saw them rape her. She had a sister. Did you ever see groups of prisoners forced to be in these positions? Where did this happen? In the showers? Did you get forced to do this, to be in this position with men? Yes. I had to do this during the three months that I was naked. Do you recognize this person? Yes, she is the female soldier who came to me and wanted to force me to have sex with her. Did you see this cloth? Did you see this cloth? Do you know where this was? Do you recognize this detainee? Do you? Did you?

dear lady of perpetual something
Contains a line (approximately) from Robert Desnos, via Franz Wright.

saudade
Contains a few lines lifted from the Frost poem "Directive," and ends with a line from Jung's *Red Book*.

[debts]

Deep thanks are offered to the editors of the following journals, and to the artists and translators I was fortunate enough to work alongside, for the time we spent together.

Alaska Quarterly Review, "jesus knew"

The American Poetry Review, "seven testimonies (redacted)"

Boston Review, "invasion of the body snatchers," "forgetting something"

Cousin Corinne's Reminder, "false prophet" and "the baffled king composing hallelujah"

Descant, "hello, birdy"

Ecotone, "self-exam (my body is a cage)"

Fence, "air"

Green Mountains Review, "kedge"

Harvard Review, "earth"

Jubilat, "haiku (failed)"

Lumina, "greetings, friend (minotaur)"

The Normal School, "dear lady of perpetual something"

Open City, "water"

Provincetown Arts, "saudade"

Sonora Review, "oh here"

Tin House, "fire," "e. corpse"

TriQuarterly, "almost song"

"fire," "air," "water," and "earth" were also published in the German edition of *The Ticking Is the Bomb* (*Das Ticken ist die Bombe*), translated by Thomas Gunkel, published by Arche Atrium, 2009.

"oh here" was written in response to the work of Louise Bourgeois, commissioned for the exhibition *Springtide,* Institute of Contemporary Art, University of Pennsylvania, Philadelphia, 2005.

"hello, birdy" was written in response to a drawing by Robert Motherwell and was commissioned for the exhibition *Ekphrasis,* Lift Truck Projects, Croton Falls, NY, 2010.

"seven testimonies (redacted)" was written in collaboration with Daniel Heyman for his Abu Ghraib paintings. "REDACTION," a limited edition artist's book, was included in the exhibition *Artists in Wartime,* Swarthmore College (and subsequently moved to Wesleyan College and elsewhere), 2010.

"seven testimonies (redacted)" and "imagination" were used in the experimental opera *Proteus,* a collaboration with the composer Guy Barash, performed by Andrew Struck-Marcell (voice), Carol Minor (keyboard), Christopher Bush (clarinet), Joey Wilgenbusch (voice), Alex Kurland (drums), Jent LaPalm (bass), Emilio Tostado (guitar), Erin Heisel (voice), Kae Reed (percussion), and Irene Fitzgerald-Cherry (violin), with video projections by Jared Handelsman and Brendan Byrne, in New York at the Galapagos Art Space and the Tank, 2010.

"imagination" was also included in the anthology *State of the Union: Fifty Political Poems,* edited by Joshua Beckman and Matthew Zapruder, Wave Books, 2008.

"imagination" was also printed as a limited edition broadside by the artist Barbara Henry for the Center for Book Arts, New York, 2009.

"e. corpse" grew out of a line given to me by Mary Jo Bang (*in the distance, in a camera flash, dolls dressed in red*), for an exquisite corpse commissioned by Brenda Shaughnessey for *Tin House,* 2010. Other poets involved in the project were Eileen Myles, D. A. Powell, Alex Lemon, and Matthea Harvey.

"saudade" is a collaboration with Mischa Richter, based on his photographs of Provincetown, Massachusetts. The collaboration is included in a limited edition artist's book, as well as being exhibited at Provincetown Art Association and Museum, Provincetown (and elsewhere), 2010.

Nick Flynn is the author of three memoirs, *The Reenactments, The Ticking Is the Bomb,* and *Another Bullshit Night in Suck City,* which won the PEN/Martha Albrand Award and was adapted to film as *Being Flynn.* He is also the author of two previous books of poetry, *Blind Huber* and *Some Ether,* which won the PEN/Joyce Osterweil Award, and a play, *Alice Invents a Little Game and Alice Always Wins.* Each spring, he teaches at the University of Houston, and then he spends the rest of the year in Brooklyn and elsewhere.

Book design by Rachel Holscher. Composition by BookMobile Design and Publishing Services, Minneapolis, Minnesota. Manufactured by Versa Press on acid-free 30 percent postconsumer wastepaper.